SCIENCE WORKS !

NUMBERS

STEVE PARKER

For a free color catalog describing Gareth Stevens Publishing's list of high-quality books and multimedia programs, call 1-800-542-2595 (USA) or 1-800-461-9120 (Canada). Gareth Stevens Publishing's Fax: (414) 225-0377. See our catalog, too, on the World Wide Web: http://gsinc.com

Library of Congress Cataloging-in-Publication Data

Parker, Steve.
    Numbers / by Steve Parker.
        p. cm. -- (Science works!)
    Originally published: Macdonald Young Books © 1995.
    Includes index.
    Summary: With a mixture of facts, experiments, and tricks,
shows how we can measure the speed of light, fly to the moon,
or buy things in a shop with only ten numbers.
    ISBN 0-8368-1964-0 (lib. bdg.)
    1. Numeration--Juvenile literature. 2. Mathematics--Juvenile
literature. [1. Number systems. 2. Mathematics.] I. Title.
II. Series: Parker, Steve. Science works!
QA141.P24 1997
510--dc21   97-10477

First published in North America in 1997 by
Gareth Stevens Publishing
1555 North RiverCenter Drive, Suite 201
Milwaukee, WI 53212 USA

This U.S. edition © 1997 by Gareth Stevens, Inc. Created with original © 1995 by Macdonald Young Books Ltd., Campus 400, Maylands Avenue, Hemel Hempstead, Hertfordshire, England, HP2 7EZ. Additional end matter © 1997 by Gareth Stevens, Inc.

Illustrators: Maltings Partnership
Picture credits: Sporting Pictures UK Ltd. 10, 27; Zefa 8, 10, 15, 22, 26, 27, 28.

Printed in Mexico

1 2 3 4 5 6 7 8 9 01 00 99 98 97

SCIENCE WORKS!

NUMBERS

STEVE PARKER

Gareth Stevens Publishing

MILWAUKEE

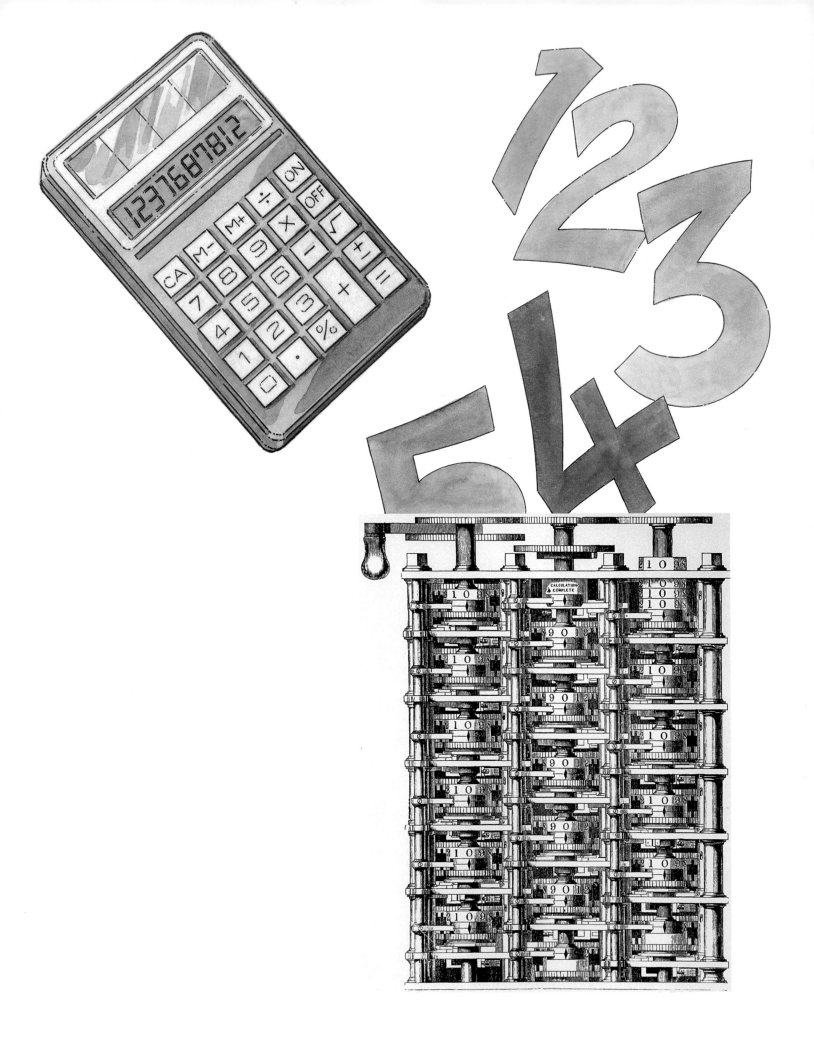

CONTENTS

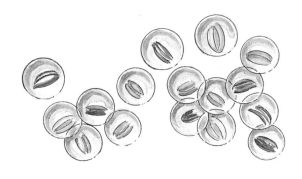

Words that appear in the glossary are in **boldface** type the first time they occur in the text.

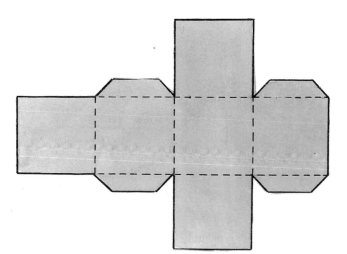

NUMBERS

Our thoughts and ideas and what we write and talk about depend on two main types of language — words and numbers. Our daily lives are full of numbers. They are not just useful for counting and doing math. We use them all the time in problem solving without realizing it. How old are you? How tall? How many brothers and sisters do you have, and how much money did you spend at the movies? What time is your favorite program on television? When is your birthday? Which is the most interesting page in this book? How much money does a millionaire have? An understanding of numbers and how to use them is vital for all kinds of science.

The story of numbers

This book looks at numbers and how people have used them through the ages, from the pyramid builders and explorers of the ancient world to the astronauts and computer programmers of modern times. Panels and boxes on almost every page present information in different ways, as explained below.

The first section of the book traces the use of numbers from early times, as shown by notches in sticks or marks on Stone Age rocks. Numbers and number systems helped the Egyptians build huge pyramids, the Greeks to think and wonder, and the Romans to conquer vast areas for their empire.

The second section describes one of the most important uses of numbers — for measuring. It also examines number systems. We use the decimal, or base 10, number system for most purposes. It is difficult to imagine any other system. But some cultures had number systems based on 20 or even 60. The binary number system in computing is based on the number 2.

The third section delves into the huge and complex area of science called mathematics. Some types of math are familiar, such as arithmetic and geometry. Others are more obscure, such as calculus and topology. But numbers and math underlie nearly all areas of science from astronomy to zoology.

In the fourth section, we look at the use of numbers and number words in daily life. These crop up in stories and rhymes, in books and movies, and in games and puzzles. How many is a "few," and is it less than "several?" Why is 13 so unlucky and 21 a cause for celebration in certain parts of the world?

The book's fifth section examines number machines, from ancient calculating aids to the latest electronic calculators and computers. The Computer Age began about fifty-five years ago, and pocket electronic calculators were not widely available until about twenty-five years ago. Imagine a world without these devices, and you will quickly understand the importance of numbers in our lives.

FAMOUS FIRSTS

Knowledge thrives on firsts, such as the first person to discover a scientific law or make an invention. The *Famous Firsts* panels describe these first achievers.

DIY SCIENCE

Follow in the footsteps of well-known scientists by trying the tests and experiments in "Do-It-Yourself" form, using everyday materials, as shown in the *DIY Science* panels.

SPECIAL FX

Scientific processes and principles can have fascinating, even startling, results. The *Special FX* projects show you how to produce these special effects. Most items are readily available in your home.

THE HISTORY OF NUMBERS

It is impossible to imagine a world without numbers. We use numbers in almost everything we do, from adding the cost of the meal we've just eaten to measuring how much we have grown to reading the sport scores, telling the time, and counting the change in our pockets. Most science involves numbers, especially one of its biggest and most fundamental branches — mathematics. A hallmark of the earliest civilizations was their use of words and numbers.

Mayan stone slab (one thousand years ago)

Arabic numbers on papyrus (one thousand years ago)

Roman polished marble (two thousand years ago)

Sumerian clay tablet (five thousand years ago)

Ancient civilizations had various symbols for writing numbers. They also wrote them on various materials, from stone and polished marble to hardened clay and early forms of paper, such as sheets of dried papyrus reeds.

Animals, as far as we know, are not aware of numbers. They do not count, add, or measure. They manage very well without numbers. So why are numbers so important in the human world?

No one knows who first used numbers. Were numbers absent from the world until they were invented by Stone Age people who counted on their fingers? Or have numbers always been there, waiting to be discovered by ancient peoples?

Notches in tally sticks and scratches on stone slabs are the earliest evidence of numbers. They date back over ten thousand years. The early use of numbers was probably for simple counting.

The first methods of recording numbers included rows of pebbles (or similar natural objects) and notches or cuts in a stick or flat stone. These slabs and tally stick (right) date back more than ten thousand years.

FAMOUS FIRSTS

THE OLDEST NUMBERS

The first numbers to be written were probably made by the Sumerians in the Middle East region known as Mesopotamia. From about 5,500 years ago, Sumerians developed a system of symbols to represent words and numerals. The symbols were made using a wooden "pencil," called a stylus, with an angled cut at one end. It was pressed into a clay tablet to produce the marks known as cuneiform writing. The clay was then baked or allowed to harden.

*Some ancient Egyptian **hieroglyphs** (picture-words and symbols) represented numbers. Many were simplified sketches of common objects, such as leaves, birds, or tools.*

NUMBERS ALL AROUND

Roman numerals are common on clock faces. For the numeral 1, Romans had **I**. For 2, they had two 1s — **II**. For 3, they had **III**. For numeral 5, they had **V**, then added 1s to it, so 6 is **VI**, 7 is **VII**, and so on. For 4, 1 was subtracted from **V** to make **IV**. For 10, with two numerals, they had one numeral — **X**. Look around in your area for examples of Roman numerals.

Roman numerals can be seen on some sundials and clock faces. They are often found on grandfather clocks.

Look at a selection of calendars and journals. You can write the date in words, such as the Third of June, Eighteen-Fifty and the Fifth of November, Sixteen Twenty-Five. You can use numerals for the day, month, and year, such as **6/3/1850** and **11/5/1625**. Some people reverse the order of the day and month, such as **4 July, 1776**.

There are various types of calendars representing the days in many different ways. The days are identified by numbers, which are called dates. The date is the number of the day in each month.

SPECIAL FX

GUESSING NUMBERS

How accurate are you at guessing the numbers of items – for example, people in a crowd or jelly beans in a jar? Many of us can develop skill at estimating numbers. Put about fifty marbles, dried beans, or similar items in a jar. Pour some out. Giving yourself just one second, try to assess how many there are. Then count the number accurately. Write down your guess and the true number. Can you improve with practice?

In a one-second glance (without counting), how many marbles are there on the right? How many are below? Most people can guess small numbers fairly accurately.

FASCINATING FACTS

- The ancient Egyptians used units of measurement based on the human arm. There were four digits (finger-widths) in a palm (hand-width) and seven palms in a cubit (from elbow to thumb-tip). The standard cubit measures 18-21 inches (524 millimeters) in today's system. Using a tape measure, what is a cubit on your own arm? The ancient Egyptians had several calendars, including the Nilotic or agricultural one based on the flooding of the Nile River, the solar calendar based on the Sun's seasonal movements, and the lunar calendar based on the Moon's phases.

- Pope Gregory XIII is best remembered for his reform of the calendar in 1582. The Gregorian calendar, named after him, is still in use worldwide today.

At first it may have been — 1, 2, more. Then people might have counted farther — 1, 2, 3, 4, 5, and so on. Counting is one of the first abstract skills we learn as young children.

The most basic type of number is a **cardinal number**. Another type is the **ordinal number**. Ordinal numbers show the order or position of things in a sequence. A common example lists winners in a competition as first, second, third, and so on.

A numeral is a symbol, mark, or shape used to represent a number. We use the modern numerals, like 1, 2, and 3 so often that we rarely think of the distinction between numbers and numerals. For example, if there is a number of cars in a row, then the numeral we might use to describe this number is 5 or the written word *five*.

An ordinal number shows position or rank in a series or sequence. We are familiar with ordinal numbers in a competition, such as first, second, and third. When standing in line, we are first, second, third, and so on.

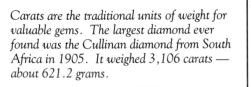

Carats are the traditional units of weight for valuable gems. The largest diamond ever found was the Cullinan diamond from South Africa in 1905. It weighed 3,106 carats — about 621.2 grams.

FAMOUS FIRSTS

A NUMBER MYSTERY

One of the first "mysterious" numbers was *pi*, usually written as the Greek letter π. It is a **ratio**, or a comparison of one number to another. The symbol π represents the length of a circle's **circumference** (all the way around it) compared to its **diameter** (across it). If you try to calculate π exactly, you would never reach the end of the calculation — π is not an exact amount, like **7** or **3**. This never-exact type of number is called an irrational number. For most purposes, we use an approximate value for π, which is **3.1412** in decimal numbers, or the fraction **22/7**. The concept of π is vital in math, geometry, mechanics, architecture, and design.

The curved line that forms a circle is called its circumference. The longest distance across the circle is its diameter. Unwind the circumference of any circle, and it is always (pi) times longer than the same circle's diameter.

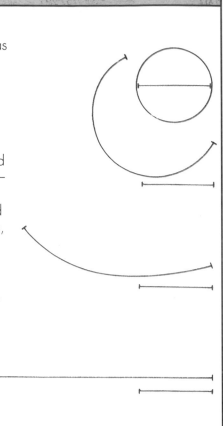

FASCINATING FACTS

- Diamonds and other precious gems are measured in units called carats. This is a traditional system based on the weight of one seed from a plant, such as the carob tree. The small pea-like seeds from this plant are all very similar in size and weight, even in plants from widely different places. So people long ago used them as standard units of weight. The word *carob* has become *carat*. The standard carat weighs 0.2 gram.

Carob plant

PUT IN ORDER — BUT WHICH ORDER?

Ordinal numbers show an order or a sequence. But you have to first decide the feature that you want to use. For example, you could put some coins in a row in order of value, from least to most valuable. Or the coins could be ranked in order of size from smallest to largest. You could also put them in order of weight from lightest to heaviest. These various sequences might differ from one another because the biggest or heaviest coins are not always the most valuable.

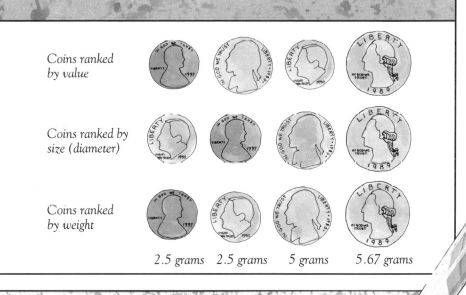

Coins ranked by value

Coins ranked by size (diameter)

Coins ranked by weight

2.5 grams   2.5 grams   5 grams   5.67 grams

NEGATIVES AND FRACTIONS

Negative numbers are minus numbers — those that are less than zero. They were probably discovered more than two thousand years ago in China, but they did not have many practical uses until the scientific revolution of the sixteenth century. Zero itself was not recognized as useful until that time. We use negative numbers in many ways, often without realizing. If you borrow money, you might write an IOU ("I owe you") note. In effect, you have a negative amount of money — less than zero. You have to pay back the amount you borrowed to go from *minus* money to *zero* money before you can have *plus* money. Can you think of other examples of negative numbers?

In cold conditions, a weather map may show negative numbers. These are temperatures that are below freezing. Outdoor thermometers have a scale showing the minus temperatures.

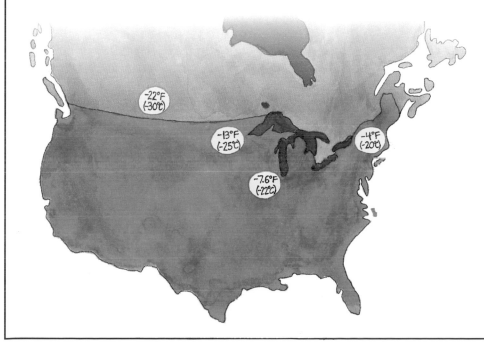

You can measure fractions by eye, guessing at one-third or one-fifth. A more accurate way is to use a protractor. This divides a circle into 360 parts or segments called degrees.

A **fraction** is a part or portion of a whole, usually shown by two numbers, one on top of the other, like three-quarters (3/4). Picture a cake. You can easily guess the fraction of one-half (1/2) of a cake by cutting the cake in two. But a fraction of three-fifths (3/5) or two-sevenths (2/7) is more difficult. Ask friends if they would prefer a slice that is three-elevenths (3/11) or one that is five-nineteenths (5/19). (The first piece is slightly larger.)

The original system of numerals began with the first writing. Over five thousand years ago, the Sumerians of southern Mesopotamia produced a type of writing called cuneiform. It used wedge-like lines and squiggles. It had simple letters, words, and numerals.

The ancient Egyptians from about five thousand years ago had a complicated system of numbers and mathematics. Numbers were used to plan, measure, organize, build, and navigate across land and sea. How many days would a journey take? How long is the side of a pyramid? How many people are in the army? Like other civilizations, the Egyptians had their own way of counting and their own numerals. For our number 1, they wrote |, which may represent a papyrus leaf. For our number 10, they wrote ∩ which could be a papyrus leaf bent over.

The ancient Greeks continued to develop numbers and mathematics. They were fascinated by the way numbers could be manipulated completely in a person's mind. For example, you could simply think of the number

The parts of an army, such as a division, brigade, battalion, or company, have a certain number of soldiers in them. The numbers have changed from one region to another and through time. In early Roman times, a centurion was in charge of 100 men — a century of soldiers. At the Battle of Waterloo in 1815 between Napoleon's French troops and those of England, Germany, Holland, and Prussia, a brigade consisted of about 800 men.

FAMOUS FIRSTS

ANCIENT GREEKS

Geometry involves using numbers to describe lines and shapes. One of the earliest and greatest mathematicians to work in geometry was Euclid of ancient Greece. He lived about 2,300 years ago. His thirteen-part book, *Elements of Geometry*, has been published in more than a thousand versions. It is one of the most widely read and admired books in science.

Euclid worked in Alexandria, a city in Egypt founded by the Greeks.

Pythagoras and his followers settled in the Greek colony of Croton, in southeastern Italy.

The first famous mathematician of the ancient world was Pythagoras. He was born on the Greek island of Samos about 2,550 years ago. Pythagoras and his followers believed in numbers so much that they said some numbers were "good," while others were "evil." They viewed the fascination of numbers as evidence of God's divine plan in creating the Universe.

DIY SCIENCE

FINDING PRIME NUMBERS

You need
Calculator, pencil, and paper.

A **prime number** is a number that cannot be divided by any whole numbers, except by itself or the number 1 *(see the boxes below)*. You can find prime numbers as follows:

1. Key a whole number, such as **6**, into a calculator.

2. Divide it by the next lowest number — in this case, **5**. Write the answer down. Then divide 6 by the next lowest number, which is **4**. Continue. If at any stage, you get an answer that is a whole number, then your starting number is not a prime number. Try other examples.

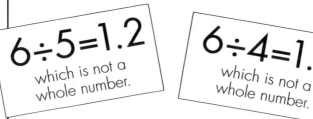

$6 \div 5 = 1.2$ which is not a whole number.

$6 \div 4 = 1.5$ which is not a whole number.

$6 \div 3 = 2$ which is a whole number, so 6 is not a prime number.

ART BY NUMBERS

Many great artists of the past knew that numbers, ratios, proportions, and geometric shapes were the basis for pleasing the eye with works of art. One of the best-known works is Leonardo da Vinci's *Vitruvian Canon of Human Proportions* (1490) shown *on the right*. He based it on the descriptions of art, proportions, and the body written by Vitruvius, an architect and writer of ancient Rome. Try your own versions using other objects, such as a dog, car, horse, or house.

Sketch a dog very quickly. Then draw a circle or square, and sketch the dog again so it fits in the shape. Is it easier to draw with the shape as a guide?

Draw a car inside a circle, square, or rectangle. Try it with a truck or motorbike.

BALANCING THE SEESAW

Using numbers, you can amaze your friends by sitting on a seesaw in the exact position to balance a friend at the other end. This is an example of a sum with two ratios. One is your weight compared to your friend's weight. The other is your distance along the seesaw compared to your friend's distance.

You need

Friend, seesaw, tape measure, calculator, bathroom scale, pencil, and paper.

1. Weigh yourself and your friend. Write down the weights.

2. Measure the distance in inches or centimeters from your friend on the seesaw to the central pivot. Multiply this by the friend's weight in pounds or kilograms.

3. Divide the answer by your own weight in pounds or kilograms. The resulting number is the distance from the pivot that you should sit.

FASCINATING FACTS

- A factor is a number that can be divided into another number to give a whole-number answer, not counting **1** and the number that is being divided. For example, the number **8** can be divided by **4 (= 2)**, or **2 (= 4)**, but not by **5** or **7**. So the factors of **8** are **4** and **2**. Does **5** have any factors?

- Factors fascinated Pythagoras and his followers. Some numbers are "perfect" because their factors add up to the number itself — **6** can be divided by **1**, **2** and **3**; and **1 + 2 + 3 = 6**. Can you find the next perfect number after **6**? (Clue — try **28**.)

- Euclid was interested in odd and even numbers. An even number can be divided by **2** to give a whole-number answer, such as **4**, **6**, **8**, and so on. An odd number cannot be divided by **2** in this way.

- Euclid believed that you could draw any geometrical shape, even very complicated ones, using only a straight-edge and a compass.

27 — you did not need 27 objects in front of you. After the Greeks, the Romans relied on numbers to organize their armies and conquer their vast empire. Their system of numerals still exists today, for instance, on clock faces. On a clock face, you may see XII. These are the Roman numerals that stand for the number 12. The numerals we use today — 1, 2, 3, and so on — are basically Arabic in origin. They came into general use in Europe from about the tenth century.

The ancient Chinese used several sets of written numerals, each for a different purpose. There were basic numerals, stick numerals on counting boards, commercial numerals for trade and bartering, and official numerals on bank notes and business contracts. Various civilizations in the Middle East, Africa, India, southeastern Asia, and the Americas developed their own number systems and numerals.

In modern life, we use numbers in almost everything we do. For example, if we are giving a party, it is helpful to know how many guests will be coming. We often use numbers to assess the size and quality of a large gathering. At a very large event, such as a parade, no one can accurately count all the people as they come and go. So estimates of crowd size often vary greatly. The police and crowd-control staff at this type of gathering may put the number at ten thousand. But the supporters of the event may say that fifty thousand people attended. Numbers can be found everywhere in our world, all the time.

Throughout the world, numbers were vital for trade and bartering and in the development of money and currency in its many forms — from seashells to peppercorns.

FAMOUS FIRSTS

COUNTING RHYMES

Most people can remember their first nursery songs and traditional rhymes from childhood. Many of these rhymes have historical origins and meanings. Rhymes often involve numbers and learning to count, such as:

One potato
Two potato
Three potato
Four
Five potato
Six potato
Seven potato
More.

One, **two**, buckle my shoe
Three, **four**, shut the door
Five, **six**, pick up sticks.

To make numbers more fun for young children, the shapes of the numerals are sometimes turned into people, animals, or objects. The public television show "Sesame Street" has many examples of this.

NUMBERS IN NAMES

Look for words based on numbers. These usually come from the Latin or Greek. Examples are words beginning with *tri*, meaning "three." *Tri* is from the Greek word *tries* and the Latin word *tres*. A tricycle has three wheels, a triangle has three sides, and a trimaran is a boat with three hulls.

A tripod fish rests on three stilt-like fins.

An octopus has eight arms.

Another example is the Latin *octo* and the Greek *okto*. These words are associated with the number eight. An octopus has eight arms, October was the eighth month in the old calendar, octane is a chemical in gasoline with eight carbon atoms, an octagon is a geometric shape with eight sides, and an octave is eight notes in the standard musical scale. What about *bi*, *quad*, *pent*, and *hex*?

HOW STEEP IS THAT?

In your travels, you may notice signs with numbers by the sides of roads and railways. These indicate the steepness of a hill or slope. The usual system is to show two numbers as a ratio. The first shows how far you go up (or down) vertically. The second refers to your travels horizontally. For instance, a slope of **1:10** shows that as you go **10** miles (or meters) horizontally, you go up **1** mile (or meter) vertically. A slope of **1:100** is much less steep than a sheer cliff of **1:0**. Another system for indicating steepness uses the degrees of a circle. A slope of **1:1** would be equal to a slope of 45 degrees.

In everyday life, the steepest slope that a car can climb is about 1:4. But mountain climbers may climb vertical 1:1 (10:10) cliff faces.

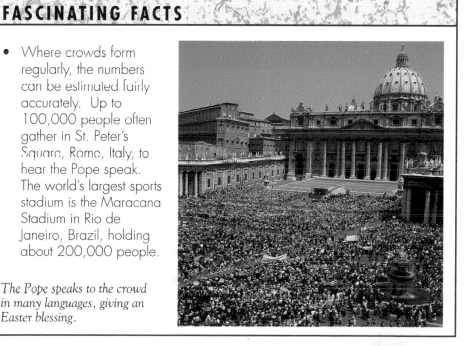

- Where crowds form regularly, the numbers can be estimated fairly accurately. Up to 100,000 people often gather in St. Peter's Square, Rome, Italy, to hear the Pope speak. The world's largest sports stadium is the Maracana Stadium in Rio de Janeiro, Brazil, holding about 200,000 people.

The Pope speaks to the crowd in many languages, giving an Easter blessing.

NUMBER SYSTEMS AND MEASURES

The temperature is about 2°F (-16.66°C). Actually, it is slightly warmer at 2.02°F (-16.65°C). This is the decimal system in action, which is used in many ways in daily life.

One of the main uses for numbers in daily life is for measuring. We measure how heavy objects are as weight. We measure distance, length, height, and temperature. We measure time with clocks.

From the beginnings of numbers and measurements, people have used many different units, such as the ancient Egyptian cubit (*see page 9*). Like numbers themselves, these units are grouped together into larger units. For example, when we measure time, we say that 60 seconds equals 1 minute, and 60 minutes equals 1 hour.

Our modern number system is based on tens. For any number, reading from right to left, the numerals indicate ones, tens, hundreds, thousands, and so on. So the number 123 indicates three 1s, two 10s, and one 100. We call this the **decimal system**. *Deci* means "ten" (*see page 15*).

There are many other number systems. In computing, the **binary system** is used. This is based on 2s, not 10s. This system is used because computers count and calculate in binary with signals of

Stopwatches measure time to fractions of a second. They are useful in athletics, particularly in racing sports.

FAMOUS FIRSTS

DECIMAL FRACTIONS
The decimal system was made popular beginning in the 1580s by Simon Stevin, or Stevinus, of Bruges, Belgium. He also shortened the method of writing fractions by making all fractions into base 10. He put commas or apostrophes above a number to show how many tenths were involved. One comma meant tenths. Two commas meant tenths of tenths, or hundredths. And so on.

139	, 6	,, 5	,,, 6	,,,, 8

Stevinus wrote decimals using commas above the fractions. This number is 139 whole units, plus six tenths, plus five hundredths, plus six thousandths, and so on.

THE DECIMAL POINT
In the 1610s, John Napier (1550-1617) suggested a quicker way of writing decimals. A dot or decimal point showed where the whole part of the number ended. Numbers after this dot would be fractions based on 10 — tenths, hundredths, thousandths, and so on. So **5.4** means 5 whole units plus 4 tenths. This did away with the commas or apostrophes proposed by Stevinus. Napier would have written the number above as **139.6568**. This system is in use today.

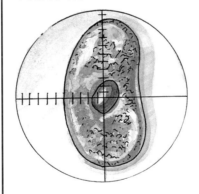

Tiny items, like this single-celled alga (plant), can be accurately measured with the aid of a microscope that contains a scale.

MEASURING VERY SMALL OBJECTS
The invention of the microscope, in about 1600, meant that people could observe extremely tiny objects such as gnats' eggs, germs, and single-celled amoebas. This opened up a whole new area for measuring very small objects. One common method is a ruler-type scale inside the microscope, which can be seen when looking through the eyepiece. You measure an object against this scale, and make a simple calculation using the magnifying power of the microscope to find the object's actual size.

DIY SCIENCE

THE DECIMAL CLOCK

We are so used to our method of measuring time, with 60 minutes in an hour and 24 hours in a day, that we rarely give it any thought. What if time measurement followed the decimal system? A clock face might have 100 minutes in 1 hour, and 10 hours rather than 12. This would mean that a 20-hour day would last **20 x 100 = 2,000** minutes. With our usual system, there are **24 x 60 = 1,440** minutes. Do you think decimal time might be more convenient?

Are you as tall as your sofa is long? It's hard to judge by just looking. Lie down next to the sofa or use a tape measure to see.

This clock looks fairly normal until you notice that the number at the top is not 12, but 10. It is a decimal clock. What is the decimal time right now?

UP AND ALONG

When we see two people standing up, we can usually estimate their heights and compare them to find out who is taller — even if the people are standing apart. We could do the same if both people were lying down. But what if one is standing and one is lying down? Most people find it difficult to compare a length from the vertical (upright) to a length from the horizontal (lying flat). This is one of many reasons why measuring distances with tools is so important.

FASCINATING FACTS

- Besides suggesting the decimal system for fractions, Simon Stevin, or Stevinus, studied the pressures in liquids, the workings of inclined planes (slopes or ramps), and a method of flooding parts of his home country by opening sluice gates to the rivers and sea to prevent invasion by enemy armies.

- John Napier invented a set of rods or strips known as "Napier's bones" for multiplying and dividing. They were an early type of calculating device. Long ago, people did not have electronic or mechanical calculators or even the manual methods of long division and long multiplication. Napier also invented the more complex idea of logarithms *(see page 10).*

SPECIAL FX

HOW MANY APPLES IS A CAR?

Most scientists and other people measure lengths with standard units, such as inches (or centimeters). But if you are measuring things solely for your own use, you can use any unit you want. How about the apple? If you have several same-sized apples, you could measure lengths and heights with them. Through the ages, people have used various units for measuring, like parts of the body *(see pages 9 and 20)*, seashells, nuts, and pebbles. But you might eat the apples or they could become rotten. Another problem with apples or similar units for measuring is that no two apples can be guaranteed to be the same size. A ruler or tape measure is more accurate and convenient.

Choose your special measuring unit, such as the apple. Measure a few objects to compare their sizes. Is it better to use a large unit, such as a watermelon, as the measuring unit, or a smaller one, such as a rice grain? For longer distances, you could use your own steps or paces. But can you always keep them the same?

To measure, you can use several same-sized units, such as apples or other objects.

electricity. No signal or "off" means 0. A signal or "on" means 1. The binary system is the simplest number system.

The ancient Babylonians used a sexagesimal system based on sixties. Reading from right to left, the numerals indicate 1s, 60s, 3,600s (60 multiplied by 60), and so on. In the sexagesimal system, our number 123 would be written as 23 — that is, two 60s and three 1s. The sexagesimal system of ancient Babylonia is the main reason why we still measure time as 60 seconds in 1 minute, and 60 minutes in 1 hour. One problem with this system is that you need sixty different numerals to go from 0 to 59. Since the modern decimal system is based on 10s, we have just ten numerals — 0, 1, 2, 3, 4, 5, 6, 7, 8, and 9. We write 59 using two numerals, not one.

We also use the decimal system for fractions, or parts of a whole. If we see the amount 2.7, we know it means two whole units plus seven-tenths of one whole unit. The decimal system and decimal fractions were pioneered by Simon Stevin or Stevinus (1548-1620), using commas above the fractions.

Long ago, people used their own units for measuring to build such structures as the Aztec and Mayan step pyramids in Central America. The Mayans used a vigesimal system of numbers based on the number 20, not the decimal system based on the number 10.

THREE SETS OF WOUNDED
During the Napoleonic wars, millions of soldiers were wounded on Europe's battlefields. Army doctors were overwhelmed with casualties. They divided the wounded into three groups — those who would die even if treated, those who would live even if not treated, and those who might die but could be saved by treatment. The doctors concentrated on the last group.

Dividing casualties into three groups is called triage (tri meaning "three"). Begun in Napoleon's time, it is still used in wars and major disasters today.

DIY SCIENCE

BASED ON TWO
The binary system of counting is based on two. It has only two numerals, **0** and **1**, and has more columns than the decimal system, as shown in the chart. This means a number that is written with only a few numerals in the decimal system, such as **127,** has many more numerals in the binary system. In fact, it has seven numerals — **1111111**. Imagine if telephone numbers were in the binary system. It would take much longer to place a call!

In the binary system, the numeral farthest to the right of a figure shows the number of ones — either 0 (no ones) or 1. The numeral to its left shows the number of twos. So the numeral 1 here means one 2 (which is 2 in base 10). The next numeral to the left shows the number of fours or 2 x 2, then eights or 2 x 2 x 2, followed by sixteens, thirty-twos, and so on. As you go left along the columns, multiply by 2 each time. The binary system is a "base 2" number system because it is based on multiples of 2.

Decimal numbers		Binary numbers			
tens	ones	eights	fours	twos	ones
	0				0
	1				1
	2			1	0
	3			1	1
	4		1	0	0
	5		1	0	1
	6		1	1	0
	7		1	1	1
	8	1	0	0	0
	9	1	0	0	1
1	0	1	0	1	0

- Another number system used in computing and computer programming is the hexadecimal system based on the number **16** *(see page 44)*. It requires sixteen numerals. Since there are only ten numerals in our decimal system, six letters are added. So the series is **0, 1, 2, 3, 4, 5, 6, 7, 8, 9, A, B, C, D, E,** and **F**. The hexadecimal number **1F** indicates one **16** and fifteen **1s**, which is equivalent to the decimal number **31**.

- The ancient Chinese used the binary number system, among others, the same system used by today's computers. The two numerals **0** and **1** are called binary digits, often shortened to the word *bits*.

OUR NUMBER	TRINARY	IMAGINARY SYSTEM
1		│
2		△
3		□
4		│ △
5		│ □
6		△ △
7		△ □
8		△ │
9		□ │ △
10		□ □
11		□ □
12		│ │ │
13		│ │

In this imaginary trinary number system, our numeral 2 is a triangle, and 3 is a square. But you could use any symbol or shape you wish!

SPECIAL FX

BINARY BRICKS

Look around for common items based on the number **2**. How about toy building blocks? Many have interlocking sets of prongs on them. The standard block is two prongs wide and two prongs long. Bigger blocks may be four or eight prongs long. This is similar to the binary system. Have you ever seen toy blocks based on a trinary system? They would be three prongs wide, and they might be three, six, nine, and so on prongs long. Games and mazes that offer a choice of two options at each stage, such as left or right, up or down, are based on the binary system.

THE TRINARY SYSTEM

Imagine a number system called trinary, similar to binary *(see opposite)*, but based on three. This means it would need three numerals, not two. Also, the columns would be based on multiples of the number **3**. The numeral on the far right would show the number of 1s. The next numeral to the left would show the number of 3s. The next numeral to the left would show the number of 9s — and so on.

THREE-WAY FIT

Measure a common house brick. It is probably about 7.5 inches long, 3.75 inches wide, and 2.5 inches high; or perhaps it is 225 mm x 112.5 mm x 75 mm. Notice that the length is twice the width and three times the height. This is no accident. It means that bricks can be stacked and interlocked neatly in many ways, even on their sides or across, with no gaps or protruding ends. The result is a wall that is both attractive and strong.

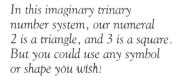

Stretcher bond

Flemish bond

The various ways of fitting bricks together are called bonds. There is space for mortar between the bricks.

Herringbone pattern

Soon after, Scottish mathematician John Napier suggested a quicker way of writing decimal fractions. After the whole number, he placed a dot or decimal point. Any numbers after this dot are fractions based on 10 with tenths, hundredths, thousandths, and so on. Napier's suggestion was not widely followed for another two hundred years, but it is now used throughout the world.

Scientists have agreed upon the use of a standard system known as the SI units, or the International System of Units. The SI is the basis for both international commerce and communication in science and technology. It is used worldwide and replaces any local system of measurement that a country uses. The seven basic units in this system are:

• **the meter** — for length or distance
• **the kilogram** — for mass (known as weight in everyday life)
• **the second** — for time
• **the ampere** — for electricity (electric current)
• **the kelvin** — for temperature (degrees K)
• **the mole** — for the amount of pure substance
• **the candela** — for brightness, or luminous intensity

From 1101 until 1824, the yard was the standard unit of length in English-speaking countries. It came from the length of Henry I's arm.

FAMOUS FIRSTS

Ballistics is the mathematical study of projectiles, such as bullets or bombs, and how they move through the air.

MEASURING EXPERIMENTS
Modern science is based on measurements made during experiments and tests. But until the seventeenth century, very few scientists did experiments or made measurements. A pioneer in this field was Italian astronomer, physicist, and mathematician Galileo Galilei (1564-1642). He introduced methods of using numbers and mathematics to calculate how objects — such as cannonballs — rolled, fell, and flew through the air. Galileo said, "The book of nature is written in mathematical numbers."

MEASURING TIME
For centuries, people had various tools for measuring time, such as marked candles or sundials, but none of these gave an exact measurement. Telling the time accurately was very important on long sea voyages. In 1759, John Harrison's fourth design of a chronometer (an accurate clock) won a major competition. It began a new era in the precise measurement of time.

Harrison's fourth chronometer was accurate to thirty seconds through an entire year, even on a swaying ship at sea.

DIY SCIENCE

UNITS OF LENGTH
There have been many different units to measure lengths over the years and in various countries. For example, horses and ponies are measured in "hands." A hand is equal to 4 inches (10 cm). In England, the distance between sets of stumps on a cricket pitch is one chain — a chain being 66 feet (20.12 meters). Do some research to find out about other measuring units, such as rods (poles or perches), leagues, and fathoms.

A chain is sometimes used to measure length.

A micrometer caliper measures accurately to 0.001 inch. Metric micrometers usually measure accurately to 0.01 mm.

MEASURING MORE PRECISELY

Scientists, engineers, machinists, and craftspeople often use special instruments to make precise measurements. Many of the instruments have a vernier scale, named after French mathematician Paul Vernier (1580-1637). A vernier scale helps measure very small distances accurately. It allows the measurement of fractions or parts of the smallest unit that can be measured on the main scale.

THE METRIC SYSTEM

The metric system was introduced in France in the 1790s. Since that time, it has been adopted as the system of weights and measures by most countries of the world, and by all countries when it comes to measurements for scientific purposes. The metric system is a decimal system based on the unit of length called the meter. The meter was originally defined as one ten-millionth of the distance from the Equator to the North Pole on a line running through Paris, France.

WHICH IS HEAVIEST?

Which is heavier, a pound (or kilogram) of feathers or a pound (or kg) of lead? The pile of feathers might look much bigger than the piece of lead, but they both weigh the same — one pound (or kg). Test this effect using kitchen scales to make same-weight piles of different substances such as flour, sawdust, pebbles, packing material, and nails. Ask your friends to guess which is heaviest.

A pile of lightweight packing material is much bigger than a pile of pebbles, so it might seem that it would be heavier. Yet the piles weigh the same.

METRIC CONVERSIONS

1 meter = 3.281 feet

1 millimeter = .0394 inch

1 centimeter = .394 inch

1 kilometer = .6214 mile

1 liter = 1.057 quarts

1 gram – .0353 ounce

1 kilogram = 2.205 pounds

1 foot = .3048 meter

1 inch = 25.4 millimeters

1 inch = 2.54 centimeters

1 mile = 1.609 kilometers

1 quart (liquid) = .9463 liter

1 ounce – 28.33 grams

1 pound = .4536 kilogram

1 gallon = 3.784 liters

To build a wall, you might use a wooden board marked in units of one brick each. In this way, it would be easy to find out how many bricks you need.

Accurate measurements are vital in space missions. A tiny error at the start could result in a spacecraft going thousands of miles or kilometers off course.

In some cases, traditional measuring units are still used for various purposes. For instance, the depth of water may be measured in fathoms. (One fathom is 6 feet or 1.8288 meters.)

Also, there may be several different sets of units for measuring the same thing. A ship's speed is measured in knots. A car's speed is measured in miles or kilometers per hour. Another object's speed can be measured in feet or meters per second. All these units measure the same thing — speed.

FASCINATING FACTS

- One way to measure wind speed is on the Beaufort scale. This was invented in 1806 by British admiral Francis Beaufort to describe how wind affects a large sailing ship. At 1 on the Beaufort scale, there is hardly any wind. At 10, there is a tremendous gale blowing that can uproot trees.

- The Richter scale was devised in 1935 by American scientist Charles Richter. It shows the strength or magnitude of earthquake shock waves. A magnitude greater than 6 on the scale is usually dangerous. The biggest earthquakes of all measure 8 or even 9. Another earthquake scale is the Mercalli scale. It uses Roman numerals, such as XII (twelve).

FAMOUS FIRSTS

A NEW GEOMETRY
French mathematician and thinker René Descartes combined **geometry** and algebra (see page 26) to create a new area of mathematics named after him — Cartesian or coordinate geometry. This revolutionized science because people could then "draw" a line using only numbers. There was no need to draw a real line with a writing instrument and paper.

René Descartes (1596-1650) was interested in many areas of science, including the links between the mind and body.

When a "human cannonball" is shot from a cannon, it is essential to know where he or she will land so a safety net can be placed there. Cartesian geometry is used to calculate the flight path.

Cartesian geometry uses the numbers and symbols of algebra to describe lines, curves, and shapes of solids. For example, a straight line on a graph is described by the algebraic formula **y = mx + c**. Descartes's methods are used in many areas of science from calculating the orbit of a comet in space to discovering the movements of tiny particles, such as the electrons in an atom. A simple example of Cartesian geometry is the graph or grid shown on the *opposite* page.

MAP NUMBERS

One familiar use of Cartesian geometry is the grid system on maps. Maps are often divided into boxes by lines going across and up-and-down. There is a series of numbers or letters or both along the side and along the top or bottom *(as in the grid below)*. To identify a box, state its location going across, then along the side. The sets of numbers and letters are called the coordinates. Maps of the world use a similar system as well as a system involving latitude and longitude. This applies parts or degrees of a circle to the sphere or globe called Earth.

A good map is clearly marked with a grid system of lines. You can pinpoint any place using the grid coordinates.

SPECIAL FX

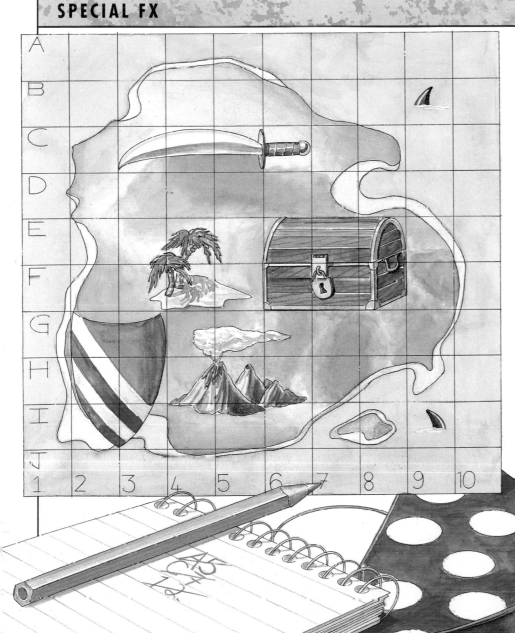

TREASURE HUNT

This game uses numbers and letters to locate the positions of objects. On a piece of paper, draw a grid or graph 10 boxes across and 10 high. Number the boxes 1-10 across and letter them A-J down. On an imaginary tropical island, hide three pieces of treasure, *as shown at left*. Your opponent does this too, but unseen by you. Dig on your opponent's island by naming a square using its coordinates, such as G3. If you hit treasure, your opponent might say, "You've found part of my shield." Take turns, digging one box at a time. If you find a part of the treasure chest, you get an extra turn. See who is first to find all of the treasure chest.

The chest is three boxes wide and two high, the shield is two boxes wide and three high, and the sword is four boxes wide.

MATH AND NUMBERS

Math is vital in almost every area of science and technology, yet it is very useful in daily life, as well. Adding and subtracting can be used to describe quantities, lines, shapes, spaces, processes, and events. We use math every time we order a fast-food lunch and every time we fill the car with gas. We use it to determine baking times for cookies and how long we have before bedtime. These are reasons why everyone learns basic math at school.

Each area of life has its special words, terms, symbols, and signs. Cooks talk about basting, blanching, and degrees. Tennis players refer to backspin lobs, serves, and love-30. Mathematics also has its language and its sets of signs and symbols called notation. The basic building blocks, or words, of math are numbers. Some parts of the notation are very familiar to us — the numerals 1, 2, 3, and so on and the symbols like **+** for plus. Other parts of mathematical notation are less familiar. You only come across these symbols when you study the subject in great detail.

Mathematics, like any broad and important subject, is divided into various areas. The most familiar is **arithmetic**. Arithmetic involves doing calculations with numbers. When you add together the cost of a day at the mall or the distance you have bicycled in one week, you are using arithmetic. There are five common symbols in arithmetic: **+** (plus or add), **−** (minus or subtract), **×** (multiply), **÷** (divide), and **=** (equals). We learn these at an early age to discover the answers to basic

Archimedes of Syracuse (287-212 B.C.) also invented weapons to defend his city against invading Romans. But he was killed in battle.

FAMOUS FIRSTS

ARCHIMEDES AND HIS PRINCIPLE

In ancient Greece, the king suspected that his new crown was not made of solid gold. Had the goldsmith mixed in a cheaper metal and kept the leftover gold? The king asked the famous scientist Archimedes to solve the problem without damaging the crown. He saw that an object placed in a fluid, such as water, weighed less — by the same weight of the amount of water it pushed aside. This is called Archimedes's principle. Using mathematics, he showed that the crown was not solid gold.

Archimedes discovered that the king's crown was not made of solid gold. It is not known whether the goldsmith was punished for his crime!

THE SAND RECKONER

Archimedes was an expert mathematician who worked with mechanical devices such as pulleys, levers, and screws. He tested and described these tools using numbers. His book *Sand Reckoner* presented new numerals, signs, and symbols to calculate with very large numbers.

He invented various devices, such as the Archimedes screw and the pulley block with numerous pulleys. Archimedes developed other useful formulas, such as how to figure the center of gravity of an object.

ON AVERAGE

Are you an average height for your age? Find out using simple math. Measure the heights in inches or centimeters of various people your age, such as the members of your class. Add all the measurements together. Divide the result by the number of people. The result is the average height. People use averages for many reasons, such as figuring the average distance a car runs on a gallon of gasoline.

MORE OR LESS AVERAGE

The everyday term *average* has a mathematical name. It is called the **mean**. We calculate the mean by adding a set of quantities or numbers, then dividing the total by the number of quantities or numbers. There are similar words used in mathematics, especially in the branch of the subject called statistics. One is the **median** — the middle number in a sequence of numbers. Another is the **mode** — the number that comes up most often. So the sequence of numbers 1, 2, 3, 4, 6, 6, 13 has a median of 4, a mean of 5, and a mode of 6.

When children line up in order of height, the person in the middle is not always an average height, but is always the median.

PASCAL AND HIS TRIANGLE

Frenchman Blaise Pascal was a brilliant mathematician, physicist, and thinker. When only sixteen years old, he was working in advanced areas of math, such as projective geometry. He used the sequence of numbers that is now called Pascal's triangle not for fun, but to begin the branch of a subject known as probability theory. This deals with the chances that events might happen, such as, "How likely will there be rain today?" Pascal also invented a calculating machine.

Pascal's triangle is made by adding two numbers next to each other on the same line, and putting the result on the line below and one space to the left.

```
              1
            1   1
          1   2   1
        1   3   3   1
      1   4   6   4   1
    1   5  10  10   5   1
  1   6  15  20  15   6   1
```

THE MAGIC SQUARE

This "magic number square" is one of many. If you add together the numbers in any single row across, or any single column top-to-bottom, or any full diagonal line, the answer is always the same. These magic squares are not found just by chance. Mathematicians have various ways of discovering which number should be in which box.

Blaise Pascal (1623-1662) was very religious. He joined a monastery at the age of thirty-two.

In this magic square, the total of the numbers in any row or column is equal to 15. Make your own magic square, three boxes high and three boxes wide, where the numbers total 9.

1	8	6
10	5	0
4	2	9

calculations, such as **2 + 2 = 4**. An understanding of arithmetic is essential in everyday life.

Geometry uses numbers to describe lines, surfaces, and shapes in space. We know many of its terms from daily life, such as circles, squares, spheres, and cubes. When we draw patterns of shapes, such as crescents or diamonds, we are using geometry. This type of mathematics is important to designers, architects, artists, sculptors, explorers, and many other people.

A third main area of mathematics is **algebra**. Algebra deals with amounts or numbers by means of general symbols, like x and y, and with finding the values of unknown numbers by calculating them from known quantities. You may use algebra without even realizing it. For example, suppose you want to visit four friends in one afternoon and spend an equal amount of time with each. You know that you have four hours and that traveling to each friend takes fifteen minutes. First, you use arithmetic. Going to four friends, at fifteen minutes each, will take sixty minutes — one hour. To find the time available for actual visiting, you subtract one hour from four hours, which leaves three hours. Using multiplication, 3 hours is 3 x 60 minutes, or 180 minutes. This time will be spread over four friends. Now, using algebra, you would say that you are going to spend x minutes with each. For four friends, that means 4x (4 times x) minutes. This 4x must equal 180. You can write this as an algebraic equation, 4x = 180. To find x, you divide each side of the equation by 4. So 4x divided by 4 is x. And 180 divided by 4 is 45. The answer can be

FAMOUS FIRSTS

TOWARD MODERN NUMBERS

Arab mathematician Al-Khwarizmi (about A.D. 800-850) introduced algebra, giving a name to one of the main branches of math. He also introduced the modern decimal system of Hindu-Arabic numerals, where the value of a number depends on its position *(see page 18)*. For example, the 1 in the number 1 means one unit. The 1 in the number 10 means ten units.

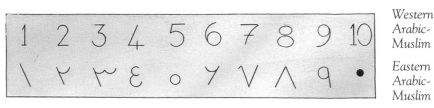

Western Arabic-Muslim

Eastern Arabic-Muslim

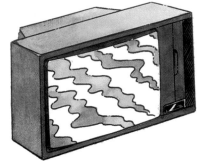

The gauss is a unit of magnetism used in electric motors and televisions. It was named after Karl Gauss.

THE ALL-AROUND MATHEMATICIAN

German Karl Friedrich Gauss (1777-1855) made astounding progress in all areas of math from arithmetic to astronomy and the calculation of the orbits of planets. His book *Researches in Arithmetic* founded the modern area of math called number theory. Gauss published few books, but he jotted down thousands of ideas and shorthand notes. Some of these complex ideas have still not been fully understood.

THE MATH OF MOVING FLUIDS

Swiss scientist Daniel Bernoulli (1700-1782) came from a family of mathematicians. He used numbers to describe the movements of gases and liquids as they flow past objects and over curves and through pipes. This branch of science is called hydrodynamics. His work is used today in many ways from calculating the lifting force of an aircraft wing to calculating the motion of water at high pressure through plumbing pipes.

You can find out how high water will spray from a fountain, such as the one below in Rome, Italy, using Bernoulli's ideas and mathematics. He showed that when water flows from a wide pipe into a narrow one, its pressure goes down — opposite of what most people believed.

ALGEBRA AROUND THE HOME

The basics of algebra can be very useful in daily life. For example, suppose you buy some chocolate bars and wish to share the squares. You decide you would like to keep twice as many squares as your best friend, and three times as many squares as your other friend. You could divide the squares like this — 3x for you, 2x for your best friend, and 1x for your other friend. Algebra helps you find the answer.

SHARE OF SQUARES

Use a letter, like x, to be the number of squares that your other friend has. You don't know what x is yet. But since your best friend is getting twice this number, he or she will have 2x squares. And you are getting three times the number — 3x squares. Add up all the shares of squares, x plus 2x plus 3x, which makes 6x. If you know that you have 24 squares altogether, then 6x = 24. To find x, divide 24 by 6, which is 4.

Let x = your other friend's share.
So $2x$ = your best friend's share.
And $3x$ = your own share.

Total shares = $x + 2x + 3x = 6x$

There are 24 squares in total.
So $6x = 24$.
This means $x = 4$.

Your other friend's share
  is 4 squares.
Your best friend's share
  is $2 \times 4 = 8$ squares.
Your own share
  is $3 \times 4 = 12$ squares.

GO WITH THE FLOW

You need
Large bowl of water, food dye.

Fill a large bowl with water. Gently add a few drops of food dye. This seeps slowly into the still water. Now stir the water gently with your hand. See how the dye follows the flow of water, moving and swirling as it spreads around. The movement may seem like a chance or random process. Yet Bernoulli's mathematics can describe what happens in detail, knowing factors such as the size of the bowl and the direction and strength of your stirring.

FASCINATING FACTS

- If you look at a wide river, you can usually see that the water in the middle flows fastest. Water near the edge goes slower because it encounters friction against the bank. So does water on the bottom, where it encounters friction on the riverbed. Boaters and sailors know this and steer their craft where the current helps them most. Computer mathematics based on Bernoulli's work can determine the exact speed of the flow under various conditions, such as during flooding due to heavy rain.

- When only three years old, Gauss checked his merchant father's accounts and found a mistake.

written as x = 45. This is how many minutes you can spend with each friend. Algebra is important to various branches of science, technology, and daily life.

There are many other areas of mathematics, and new ones have been developed through the ages. One of the most brilliant scientists of all time, Englishman Sir Isaac Newton (1642-1727), invented the type of mathematics called **calculus**. Calculus deals with amounts and quantities that change with time, such as "What's the speed of a car accelerating at the start of a race? It's 10 miles (km) per hour . . . no, it's 20 miles (km) per hour . . . wait, now it's 30 miles (km) per hour." The speed of the car changes with each fraction of a second. Calculus is a type of math that allows calculations of these changing quantities. Calculus is vital when working with machines, mechanical devices, and crafts of all kinds from boats to space rockets.

A beehive contains rows of six-sided cells. Young bees develop in them as eggs and grubs. Honey is also stored in them. The hexagon-shaped design lets the bees use as little material as possible to enclose the greatest space possible — a perfect example of natural geometry.

FAMOUS FIRSTS

SCIENCE BY MATH

James Clerk Maxwell (1831-1879) did some scientific experiments, but his main tool for exploring science was mathematics. Using calculations, he found that light rays were a small part of an entire range of waves called the electromagnetic spectrum. He also predicted how to make radio waves. This finding opened the way for Hertz and Marconi to begin the age of radio and television.

Maxwell made many advances in physics, including the study of high-temperature, high-pressure gases in engines.

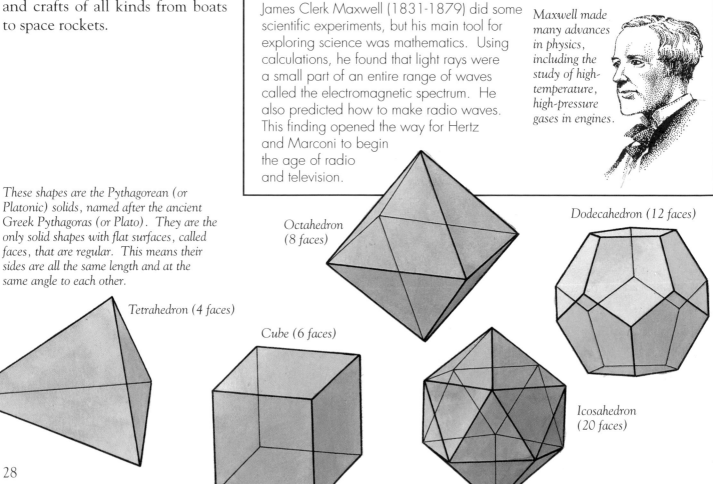

These shapes are the Pythagorean (or Platonic) solids, named after the ancient Greek Pythagoras (or Plato). They are the only solid shapes with flat surfaces, called faces, that are regular. This means their sides are all the same length and at the same angle to each other.

Tetrahedron (4 faces)

Cube (6 faces)

Octahedron (8 faces)

Icosahedron (20 faces)

Dodecahedron (12 faces)

FOLDED FROM FLAT

Look at the flat pattern on the right. Think about cutting it out and folding along the broken lines. What would be the result? In your mind, picture doing this task, and visualize the solid shape that would form. There are clues as you look at the pattern — it has six sides, and each side is a square. In the same way that people manipulate numbers in the mind, this is another mind-based type of mathematics called "mental geometry." Can you think of other ways to draw the flat pattern to get the same result? Many people, such as designers and builders, get used to manipulating patterns and shapes in their minds. The art of folding paper, known as origami, also uses the same mental processes.

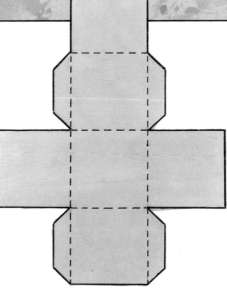

Flat shapes that fold into three-dimensional shapes are called nets.

The planets, including our Earth, orbit in ellipses around the Sun.

CURVES AND MORE CURVES

You need
String, two pins, pencil, paper.

An **ellipse** is a curved shape with two centers called foci (plural of focus). The distances from any one point on the ellipse to focus "A" and focus "B" always add up to the same number. Draw an ellipse, as shown. Loop string around the pins that form the foci. Place a pencil inside the loop anywhere on the ellipse. Moving the pencil to other points on the ellipse will use the same amount of string, even when the lengths to each focus change.

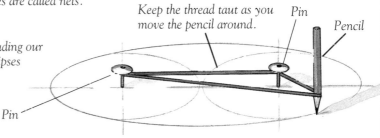

Keep the thread taut as you move the pencil around. Pin — Pencil

Pin

JUDGING AREAS

It is fairly easy to judge and compare lengths. If you were shown two lines side by side, you could probably determine the longer one. Comparing the areas covered by shapes is also not hard if the shapes are similar — for instance, if they are both circles. If you were shown two circles of different sizes, you could probably say which is bigger. It is more difficult to compare areas when their shapes are different. For instance, look at the shapes on the right. Which has the largest area?

The accurate way to find which shape has the largest area is to measure them, using the mathematics of geometry to calculate the areas. For each shape, there is a mathematical formula that determines the area. For a square, this is the length of one side multiplied by itself, since all sides are the same length. For a rectangle, it's the longer side multiplied by the shorter side. For the circle, it is the **radius**, **r** (the distance from the center to the circumference) multiplied by itself and then by pi, π *(see page 10)*. This is written as πr^2.

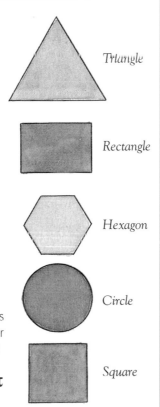

Triangle

Rectangle

Hexagon

Circle

Square

- The Arab scholar Omar Khayyam (1048-1122) wrote about numbers and math. He helped distinguish arithmetic from algebra. He also used the device now known as Pascal's triangle *(see page 25)* — hundreds of years before Pascal! Omar Khayyam was an astronomer, too. From his observations of the Sun, Moon, and stars, he developed a new calendar. But he is perhaps best known for his poetry, the *Rubai'yat*.

- Pascal's triangle was also recognized by both Chu Shi-Chieh, a Chinese mathematician, and Halauydha, a mathematician in ancient India, 1,300 years before Pascal.

Calculus caused a major scientific argument at the time. The German mathematician Gottfried Leibniz (1646-1716) also developed calculus, and Newton accused him of stealing the ideas. Supporters of the two great scientists did not speak to each other for many years.

A common form of mathematical notation is known as *percent*, represented by the symbol %. It means "per 100." If 59% of people like a certain flavor of ice cream, this means 59 people out of 100 like the flavor. If you asked 1,000 people if they liked the ice cream, then 590 might say yes. Sometimes percentages can be changed to fractions, or the other way around. For instance, 50% means 50 out of 100 (50/100). This can be simplified to 5 out of 10, or 1 out of 2. That's the same as one-half, or 1/2.

Architects and designers use various types of mathematics, especially arithmetic and geometry, to draw plans and blueprints for buildings and other structures.

FAMOUS FIRSTS

MAKING π MORE ACCURATE

The number called pi, **π**, is explained on page 10. Through the ages, various people have used different values for it. For the ancient Hebrews, **3** was close enough. Ancient Egyptians and Greeks, such as Pythagoras, used **22/7**. One of the earliest attempts to give **π** an accurate value was in ancient China around 500 B.C. when it was calculated as **355/113**.

DIY SCIENCE

MAKE YOUR OWN PI

You need

A compass, pencil, paper, pin, thin thread, ruler.

Calculate your own value for the mysterious number pi, **π**.

1. Draw a circle with a compass. Measure its radius (the distance from the center to the circumference) with a ruler.
2. Pin the end of the thread to one point on the circumference. Then carefully place the thread all the way around the circle, back to the pin.
3. Straighten this length of thread, and measure it with a ruler.
4. Divide the length of thread (the circumference) by twice the length of the radius. Is your answer near the usual value of pi, **3.1412**?
5. Draw a much larger circle, and make another measurement of pi, **π**. Does this larger circle give you a more accurate value for pi?

NUMBERS FOR VOLUMES

Liquids are usually packaged and sold by volume. Find containers of various liquids, such as mineral water, sparkling grape drink, milk, juice, paint, soda pop, perfume, and dishwashing soap. Put them in a row, and guess which holds the most.

Now look at the labels to find the volume that each one contains. Can you be tricked by the shape and design of a container into thinking it holds more than it does?

DIY SCIENCE

THE PROBLEM WITH VOLUMES

You need
Large bowl, small glass, water.

We can compare and judge lengths fairly easily. Areas are more difficult *(see page 29).* Turning volumes into numbers and comparing them is usually even more difficult. Observe a large bowl, and compare it to a small glass. How many times will you have to fill the glass with water and empty it into the bowl to fill the bowl? Take a careful guess. Then find out the number of glasses by actually doing the experiment. Were you correct? Ask others to take a guess. How many glasses fill the bowl? It might be many more than one would think. Most people estimate low.

SPECIAL FX

LEARN ABOUT NUMBERS AND QUANTITY

You need
Two large clear glasses, a taller but thinner clear glass or beaker, water, several young children (2-3 years old), and people of various ages (3 years old and up).

From an early age, children learn to count and do simple addition. But dealing with volumes is trickier. Do the experiment below with the cooperation of a range of people, from young children to adults. Younger children make comparisons about area and volume in a simple way. Many children (up to about five years old) guess that, in step 3, the tall thin beaker holds the most water. This is because the water's surface is higher when compared to the shorter, wider glass. Young children make the comparison by length or distance. Yet they have already seen the same amount of water in the shorter, wider glass and understood that the two volumes of water are the same. Try the comparison in step 3 on older children and adults.

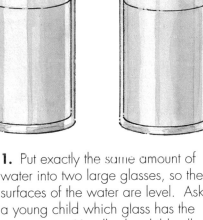

1. Put exactly the same amount of water into two large glasses, so the surfaces of the water are level. Ask a young child which glass has the most water. Usually, the child will reply that they are both the same.

2. While the young child watches, pour water from one large glass into a taller, thinner beaker. (Check beforehand that the taller container can hold the amount of water.)

3. Now ask the child again which container has the most water? Younger children often reply that the taller one contains the most because its surface is higher.

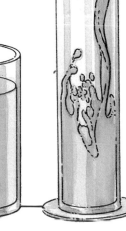

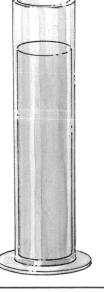

NUMBERS IN FICTION, FACT, AND FUN

Cats can survive falls that would injure or kill most other animals. They survive because of their sharp senses, agility, and quick reactions, turning in mid-air to land safely. This brought about the saying, "A cat has nine lives."

I n daily life, we use numbers in a less strict way than measuring and doing technical calculations. A number might be in an old saying or rhyme. Does a cat really have nine lives? The number might be in the title of a book, song, or film. Or you might use a number to give an impression or to exaggerate. Have you really been told a million times to tidy your bedroom? These numbers are not supposed to be accurate. They are part of everyday language.

Do bad-luck events really come in threes? Or is it more a case of "third time's a charm?" If you break a mirror, you may have seven years of bad luck. But if you are the seventh son of a seventh son, you are supposed to be very lucky. What is so special about the number 21 and 25 and events such as a person's 21st birthday or 25th wedding anniversary? And why is 13 considered so unlucky in some parts of the world?

Numbers crop up all the time in legends, fables, folklore, and traditional songs and rhymes. Sometimes these stories have explanations. Starting long ago, many items were packed or supplied in groups of 12, called dozens. Receiving one more than a dozen, 13, meant that someone else was one short. If they found out that you had the extra one, you might be in trouble!

There has been a long and fascinating relationship between words and numbers. Some words indicate that we do not mean an exact number, but something

FAMOUS FIRSTS

PIONEERS WITH NUMBERS

Leonhard Euler (1707-1783) of Switzerland wrote more books and scientific articles than any other mathematician in history. He lost the sight in one eye, perhaps by looking at the Sun during his astronomy studies. Later, he became totally blind, but he continued his work due to his amazing ability at mental arithmetic. A notation in math — **e** — (Euler's number) is named after him.

Frenchman Jules Henri Poincaré (1854-1912) worked in many areas of mathematics, such as **topology**, which is a branch of geometry that deals with how objects change when bent, twisted, and turned inside out. Poincaré also advanced other areas of science regarding the orbits of the planets, the effects of gravity, and the movements of electrons and other particles inside atoms.

Albert Einstein was one of the most brilliant mathematicians and scientists of all time. He changed many areas of science with his **theory of relativity**. It is written as lists of numbers and symbols. This continued Sir Isaac Newton's work and is a cornerstone of modern science, particularly involving events in outer space and deep within the atom.

Albert Einstein (1879-1955) was a brilliant scientific thinker.

DIY SCIENCE

NUMBERS IN NAMES

Look for numbers that appear in the names of songs, rhymes, books, stories, and movies. How about *101 Dalmatians* or *Ali Baba and the Forty Thieves*? Do certain numbers crop up again and again, especially in traditional tales? For example, how many dwarfs befriended Snow White, how many seas did sailors sail, and how many brides married how many brothers?

Did you manage to spot all of the dalmatians in Walt Disney's famous animated movie?

NUMBERS AND SUBSTANCES

Some numbers are associated with substances. Find a reference list of birthdays or anniversaries. What is a golden wedding anniversary or a silver jubilee? As the number increases, the substance usually becomes more valuable. So diamonds and gold are linked with larger numbers. In modern times, however, substances such as titanium might be quite high on the list.

GOING ON FOREVER?

The quantity called infinity *(see above right)* might seem to go on forever. But almost any process or sequence that you think could go on forever has some kind of limit. An example: "How many times could you fold a newspaper in half?" In theory, the number of folds is limitless. But after a few folds, the paper would be too thick to fold any further.

SPECIAL FX

HOW BIG IS INFINITY?

The quantity known as **infinity** *(see page 38)* is shown by the symbol ∞. It is sometimes said that infinity is unlimited — it goes on forever and is a number so huge that it has no end. But mathematics puts a limit on infinity. It is defined as "a quantity that is greater than any assignable quantity." Infinity is bigger than any quantity or number you can think of, but it is not endlessly large. You can also have minus infinity, which has the symbol -∞.

In this painting by Maurits Escher, things do not seem to become infinitely small with distance. This produces a confusing effect.

FASCINATING FACTS

- In 1954, English athlete Roger Bannister was the first to run the mile in less than four minutes. The "four-minute mile" seemed to break an important barrier. Yet, it was only one record in a continuing series of records.

- Sports records go up in small amounts. But breaking a round number, like scoring 100 points or playing in 100 games, seems to be more of an achievement.

No matter how big your sheet of paper — even if it were the size of Africa — you would reach a point where no more folds are possible because of the thickness.

near — like *approximately, around, about, nearly, almost,* and *roughly.* The Chinese mathematician and astronomer Chongzhi Zu, who calculated the value π (pi) *(see page 30),* lived in ca. 429–500. The *ca* stands for *circa,* a Latin word that means "about" or "approximately," since we are not sure of his exact life span.

Other words represent quantities that are general, not exact. They include *few, several, many,* and *lots.* If you had a few apples in a bowl, how many would that be — 2, 3, 4, maybe more? What about several apples in the bowl — 5, 6, 7, or perhaps more? As the quantities get larger, they become more vague. If you saw hundreds of people at a large event, no one would expect that you saw exactly 200, or 300, or another precise number of hundreds. It could even be thousands, but hundreds gives the general impression. There are also words for exact quantities, such as a *dozen* (12) or a *gross* (144). These come mainly from older measuring systems.

DIY SCIENCE

THE GOLDEN SECTION
Certain shapes and proportions please our eyes. Since ancient times, designers, architects, and artists have studied the numbers and measurements behind these proportions and ratios. One is the golden section or golden ratio. It is used to design buildings and to calculate the sizes and positions of objects, such as paintings on a wall or flower beds in a garden.

Throughout history, designers have used the balanced proportions of the golden section to design structures, including the Parthenon in Athens, Greece.

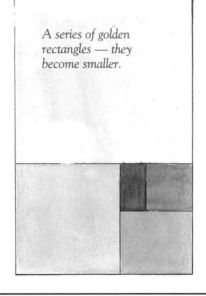

A series of golden rectangles — they become smaller.

You need
Large sheet of paper, pencil, ruler.

In a golden rectangle, the comparison or ratio of the long side to the short side is the same as the sum of the long and short sides to the long side. Draw a rectangle about 6.5 inches (16.2 cm) by 4 inches (10 cm). The long-to-short comparison is 6.5 (16.2) divided by 4 (10), which is about 1.62 (the golden section). The both-sides sum to the long-side comparison is 10.5 (26.2) to 6.5 (16), also about 1.62.

The White House in Washington, D.C., is the official residence of the president of the United States. It was designed in the classical style, using numbers such as the golden section, or ratio.

The palace of Versailles, near Paris, France, is another beautiful building whose proportions are not accidental. The proportions were calculated carefully to give the impression of harmony and elegance.

FASCINATING FACTS

- Italian stone-carver Andrea Palladio (1508-1580) was one of the best-known architects of the Renaissance period. His work on shapes, measurements, and proportions was based on the architecture of ancient Rome. He often utilized the numbers 3 and 1.62 (the golden section).

- Palladio founded a style of architecture that was named after him. Buildings in the Palladian style, such as those shown *opposite*, grace many cities around the world.

DIY SCIENCE

USING THE GOLDEN SECTION
Can you design a building using numbers, such as the golden section and the Fibonacci sequence? It could be old-fashioned or modern, a temple or a church, a library, a school hall, a hotel, or a skyscraper. Sketch the general design first, without measuring. Then use numbers to design more exactly the overall height and width, and also the shapes and positions of columns, girders, windows, and doors.

SPECIAL FX

THE FIBONACCI SEQUENCE
Italian mathematician Leonardo Fibonacci (about 1170-1250) helped introduce the Hindu-Arabic system of numbers to Europe. He also discovered a series of numbers where the next number is found by adding the two previous numbers — 1, 1, 2, 3, 5, 8, 13, and so on. This Fibonacci sequence is often found in measurements of natural patterns, such as the growth of a tree's branches or a deer's antlers. Draw a tree. Then draw another, based on branch measurements using numbers from the Fibonacci sequence.

The Fibonacci sequence is commonly found in nature.

SPECIAL FX

MUSIC BY NUMBERS
You can use numbers to compose a tune. On a keyboard instrument such as a piano, the musical scale goes up in sets of eight white keys. Write down a sequence of numbers between 1 and 8. Choose any white key as number 1, and play the number sequence. Is it a pleasing tune? Repeat the tune, choosing another white key as number 1. Does the tune sound different? With the note called middle C as number 1, what does the sequence 1155678654433221 sound like?

We also see numbers on signs. Some signs announce age limits — for instance, "Those under 18 are not admitted." Road signs announce the speed limit. Warning signs may restrict the width of vehicles or show a weight limit.

Ancient people did not have the number zero with its numeral 0 or Ø *(see page 8)*. What would be the point of describing nothing at all? Aristotle likened numbers to a heap of objects, so if there were nothing in the heap, there could be no number for it. Yet zero has a vital place in all modern mathematics. The idea of zero was used in ancient Chinese mathematics. It also appeared in ancient India. From the eighth century, zero gradually made its way to Europe, helped by Arab mathematicians, such as Al-Khwarizmi. The Mayan people of Central America also had zero in their number system.

At the opposite end of the number scale is the quantity called infinity, with the symbol ∞. If you started counting 1, 2, 3, 4, and so

On a map, contour lines represent numbers — usually the height of the land above sea level. The closer the lines, the steeper the slope.

FITTING SHAPES TOGETHER

Tessellations are regular, repeated shapes that fit together exactly, without gaps. We see them on mosaics, on tiled floors and walls, on fabrics and curtains and wallpaper, and in jigsaws. Escher *(see page 33)* developed some artistic tessellations by using numbers and measuring the patterns exactly. Could you devise a series of tessellations? Base them on a number or regular shape, such as a triangle or hexagon.

This pattern by Escher shows birds in flight, merging into fish in the water, forming a tessellation.

PEOPLE TOGETHER

The next time you attend a big event, study how the seats are arranged in rows and tiers. Each seat has certain measurements — width, depth, leg-room, and the height of the seat behind. Designers calculate how the seats fit together, so that the site holds as many people as comfortably possible, allowing for the various aisles, stairs, corridors, and exits. Similar calculations show how many tables and chairs fit into a cafe or restaurant.

Wallpaper usually repeats its pattern at least once across each strip. Measure across the repeat distance. Is it the same as the repeat distance up or down the strip?

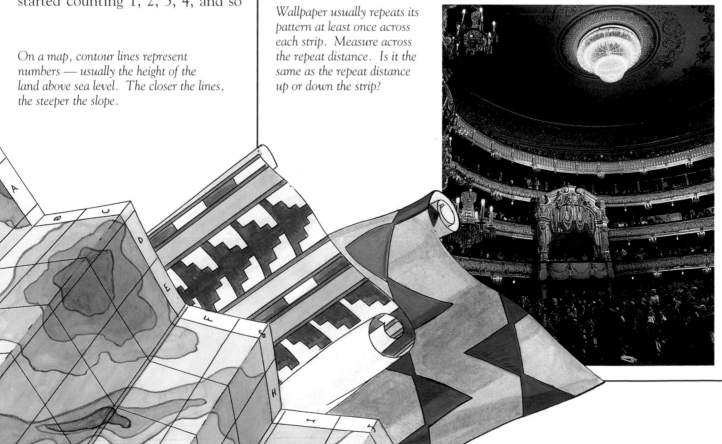

THE PARADOXES OF ZENO

In ancient Greece, the thinker Zeno argued about movement and change. His paradoxes are puzzles that seem to be either true or false, but the opposite happens. For example, Greek hero Achilles raced a tortoise, giving it a head start of 10 miles (km). For each distance Achilles ran, the tortoise moved one-tenth of this distance. Achilles ran 10 miles (km), and the tortoise moved 1 mile (km). Then Achilles ran 1 mile (km); the tortoise moved 0.1 mile (km). Does Achilles ever catch his slow opponent?

In Zeno's paradox, the tortoise always stays in front, but by an ever-decreasing distance.

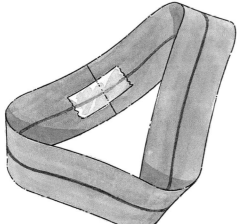

A ring shape made from an untwisted ribbon has two surfaces, inside and out. The Möbius strip (left) has a twist in it, and so it has only one surface. This is called a topological paradox.

THE MÖBIUS STRIP

The Möbius strip is named after German mathematician August Möbius (1790-1868). It can be drawn in two dimensions or made as a three-dimensional model *(see below)*. The Möbius strip has some unusual features as explained by the branch of mathematics known as topology *(see page 32)*.

THE TWISTED STRIP

You need
long, thin strip of paper; scissors; pen; tape.

1. Hold the strip straight, twist one end by a half-circle (in numbers, 180°). Tape the two ends together. The result is a Möbius strip.

2. The strip has only one surface or side. Show this by drawing along its middle. Start anywhere — and you return to the same spot, without taking pen from paper.

3. With scissors, carefully cut along the line you drew. Do you get two separate strips, or two joined ones, or one long strip? How many twists are there?

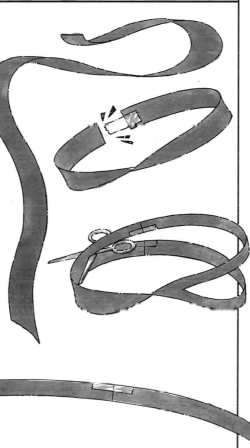

- Leonhard Euler was so fascinated with mathematics that he was working on numbers even on the day he died. At that time, he was calculating how fast the recently invented hot air balloon would rise.

- The idea for the Möbius strip was only discovered after the death of its inventor, August Möbius, when others collected and read his notebooks and papers.

- Möbius also suggested the five-color problem described on page 30.

- The study of tessellations has produced many unusual designs for bricks, so that buildings made from them can each look different. Are there any buildings like this in your area? Tessellations also help in the design of tile patterns and mosaics.

on, and you could count forever, would you ever reach the end? No, the series of numbers goes on forever. But this is not quite the same as infinity. The quantity infinity is greater than the size of anything you can think of, that is, any other limited number (*see page 33*). This makes infinity a more useful idea in math. There are also special numbers called **constants**. These are always the same. An example is pi, π. One of the best-known and most useful constants is the speed of light. It is measured at 186,290 miles (299,792 km) per second, and it is always the same wherever you are in the Universe.

Numbers are also familiar in competitions and games of chance, such as lotteries, raffles, and drawings. When buying a lottery ticket, some people like to use numbers derived from the ages, birthdays, and other statistics of family members and friends. However, if the drawing or competition is truly random in the way the numbers are selected, then every number has an equal chance of coming up. So it really does not matter which numbers you choose or whether you keep the same ones or change them each time. Similarly, if you toss a coin five times and it shows "heads" each time, then the likelihood of the sixth toss being "heads" or "tails" is still 1 to 1. It is not 5 to 1 because the preceding results do not affect the situation. Over many tosses, the results even out. There is a saying, "Chance has no memory."

FAMOUS LASTS

SOLVED AT LAST?
In his spare time, French government law officer Pierre de Fermat learned languages, wrote poetry, and researched math. He made many advances in the study of probability (*see below*), in the shapes of curves, and in how light is bent by lenses. In 1637, he wrote an equation that became known as "Fermat's last theorem." It wasn't solved until the 1990s.

DIY SCIENCE

WHAT ARE THE ODDS?
Have you ever entered a chance event like a lottery, raffle, or sweepstakes? What are the "odds" of your winning? The odds are the chance that you will win compared to the chance that you will not. If a lottery has ten numbers, and you choose one, then the odds that you will win are 1 - 9 (one-to-nine). If you choose nine numbers, the odds are 9 - 1. Look for examples of odds and how they are calculated, such as in lotteries and betting on horse races and other events.

100,000,000,000,000,00

WRITING HUGE NUMBERS
In a truly enormous lottery, the odds against you winning are extremely large. It can take a long time to write such huge numbers using standard numerals. So mathematics has a shorthand way of showing them. It makes use of another number that is written smaller and higher than the main number. This number shows how many times the main number is multiplied by itself and is referred to as the "power." 10^6 (10 to the power of 6) is 10 times 10 times 10 times 10 times 10 times 10, which equals 1,000,000, or one million. What does 10^{20} equal? It is written out fully *above*.

- Another version of Zeno's paradox *(see page 37)* concerns a frog hopping across lily pads from one side of a pond to the other. Its first jump covers half the distance, and each following jump is half as long as the previous one. So the second jump gets the frog three-quarters of the way across, then seven-eighths, and so on. Does the frog ever reach the other side?

- Using the decimal system, some numbers cannot be written exactly. For example, the quantity one-third can be written exactly as the fraction, **1/3**. But in the decimal system, it is **0.3333333**. In theory, these 3s go on forever, never reaching the end. It is called an indeterminate number. To help this situation, the symbol **r** can be used. The **r** stands for "recurring," occurring again and again. The decimal for one-third is **0.33^r**.

The betting odds are displayed as numbers at the racetrack. The lowest or shortest odds, like 2-1 or 3-1, indicate the favorite — the horse which most people think will win.

SPECIAL FX

MORE THAN FOUR?

The mosaic or map paradox, also called the five-color problem, has long puzzled mathematicians and artists. The challenge is to find a design where five colors are needed to fill in the shapes, so that no two colors touch. No one has yet succeeded because four colors always seem enough. Can you solve the problem? Draw a map or mosaic using any shapes you wish. Or trace and color the mosaic above. Color it so that no neighboring shapes are the same color. Are four colors enough?

NUMBER MACHINES

Numbers are used all the time in today's world, but we do not have to manually manipulate numbers as much as in days gone by. In the past, people had to do calculations with pen and paper. Shopkeepers, merchants, accountants, engineers, metalworkers, carpenters, and more all had to do math by hand. Lengthy problems took days. Much of this work is now done by calculators, computers, and other devices. Many complex calculations are accomplished in less than a second.

There are many types of machines that do calculations and mathematics. Look at a modern calculator. It has the numerals 0 to 9, and arithmetic signs, such as +, −, x, and ÷. It also has many other buttons. Many of these buttons are used for complicated work. They are useful for all types of science from math and physics to biochemistry and ecology. The idea of devices to record and manipulate numbers actually comes from ancient times.

There are many kinds of number machines. When does a memory aid become an adding machine, which then becomes a computer? Memory aids are very simple — they record or store

Warplanes showed the number of their victims with painted lines. After four lines, the fifth was indicated by another line through them. This resulted in units of five, which were easier to total.

FAMOUS FIRSTS

TOWARD THE POCKET CALCULATOR
When he was nineteen, Blaise Pascal *(see page 25)* invented a machine to do addition and subtraction. He wanted to help his father in business. He sold these adding machines to help with the family income. This part of Pascal's scientific work is remembered by the computer programming language named after him.

The slide rule was a forerunner of the pocket calculator. The central portion could slide along, doing complex multiplication and division.

Charles Babbage (1792-1871)

NAPIER'S LOGARITHMS
In the years before inventing his "bones" in 1617 *(see page 17)*, John Napier devised a new way to multiply. He did it by converting numbers to another form, called the logarithm. To multiply two numbers, you would add their logarithms. Napier produced large tables of logarithms. Sliding scales, called slide rules, based on the tables accomplished the calculations easily. This made multiplication simple.

BABBAGE'S ENGINE
English scientist Charles Babbage wanted to invent a calculating machine to take the drudgery out of mathematics. He worked on designs using gears and levers. His first version was completed in 1833 and was called the difference engine. It could find the logarithms of numbers. Babbage went on to design various versions of an analytical machine. These machines were not built due to lack of money and engineering skills. But they had several features of the modern computer, such as a program (a card with holes punched in it) and memory.

Babbage's analytical machine (opposite) might have been able to reduce the drudgery of manual calculations, but it was never built.

DIY SCIENCE

MAKING AN ABACUS

The abacus is mainly a memory aid, showing a number in a physical form. An abacus can show numbers by the positions of beads on wires. In one common version, there are rows of five beads (representing ones) below the center, and rows of two beads (representing fives) above the center. On the right-hand wire, three beads slid up in the lower portion means 3. One bead slid up in the upper portion means 5. With the 3, the total is 8. The next wire to the left is tens, then hundreds, and so on.

You need
Cardboard, old sponge, five thin wooden dowels, glue, scissors.

1. Cut cardboard strips, as shown, to make a shallow box, about 16 inches (40 cm) by 12 inches (30 cm) and 3 inches (8 cm) deep. Also cut out a central partition for the box, as shown.

2. Carefully cut up an old sponge into about fifty small, ball-shaped lumps that are slightly larger than grapes.

3. Punch five equally spaced holes in the box's central partition. Push the dowels through. Thread on the balls of sponge. For this abacus, put five balls on one side of the partition and five on the other.

4. Assemble the box, as shown, and glue it together. Each of the five rows has 10 balls representing simply the numbers 1-10. How would you record the number 4? 7? 10? 23? 147? 6,377?

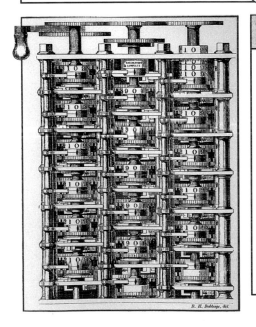

SPECIAL FX

CLOCKING UP DISTANCES

There is a simple adding machine in vehicles, such as cars, trucks, and motorcycles. It is called the odometer. It counts the number of miles or kilometers the vehicle has traveled. If you could take apart an old one, you would see the system of toothed gears that turns around and advances the numbered wheels. Each time a wheel turns around once, from 0 to 9 and then 0 again, the wheel to its left moves one position. In this way 00999 becomes 01000.

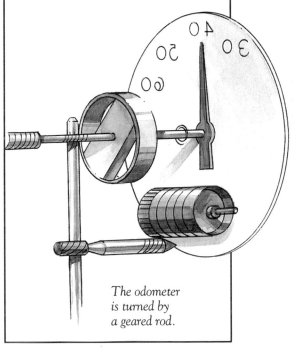

The odometer is turned by a geared rod.

FASCINATING FACTS

• Charles Babbage's analytical engine would have been the first proper computer, although it was mechanical, not electronic. He continually changed the plans for the engine, trying to improve it. So it was never completely finished.

• Ada Lovelace, daughter of the poet Lord Byron, assisted Babbage in his work. The computer programming language called ADA, used by the United States Department of Defense, is named after her.

• As Babbage ran out of funds, he tried to invent a successful mathematical system for winning money by placing bets on horse races. But the system failed.

numbers, usually according to the position of physical objects. Examples are rows of pebbles in sand, notches on a counting stick, or knots on a string.

Slightly more complicated devices include the abacus. The abacus stores numbers while the operator carries out a calculation. It cannot do calculations itself; the operator must know how to use it. So it is really a calculating or computing aid. In ancient times, the abacus consisted of rows of pebbles in grooves in the earth. The Greeks turned it into a portable device, the abax, by making grooves or drawing lines on a board or slate. The name *abacus* is now linked to the Chinese version, the suan p'an, with rows of beads strung on rods or wires in a frame.

In ancient Greece, Hero of Alexandria described a machine that could add the distances traveled by a wheeled cart or carriage. It worked using gear wheels with pegs on them. This device was the first automatic counter. Modern versions of this are found in cars and other vehicles. It is the distance recorder, called the odometer.

Space flights would be impossible without computing power to test, check, operate, and control all the systems and equipment.

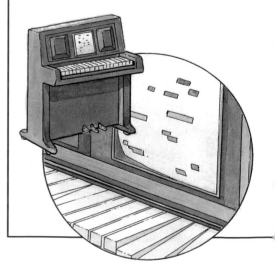

A computer needs devices that let it input information and get the information back again after it has been processed. Input devices include the keyboard, mouse, magnetic disk drive, compact disc, magnetic tape, scanner, microphone, and digital camera. Output devices include the monitor screen, printer, magnetic disk drive, magnetic tape, and loudspeaker. Computers can send information, in the form of binary numbers, among themselves along telephone cables, using a modem (modulator-demodulator).

- When dealing with large numbers, several numerals are required. For example, one million has six zeros — 1,000,000. Scientists use letters and prefixes to make writing huge numbers easier:

Symbol	Prefix	Numbers before Decimal point	Words
T	Tera-	13	Trillions
G	Giga-	10	Billions
M	Mega-	7	Millions
k	Kilo-	4	Thousands
h	Hecto-	3	Hundreds
da	Deca-	2	Tens

So 1 gigawatt of electricity produced by a fairly large power station can be written as 1 GW, 1 billion watts or 1,000,000,000 watts.

- The same happens with parts of whole numbers:

Symbol	Prefix	Numbers before Decimal point	Words
d	Deci	1	Tenths
c	Centi-	2	Hundredths
m	Milli-	3	Thousandths
k	Micro-	6	Millionths
µ	Nano-	9	Billionths
p	Pico-	12	Trillionths

- The size of the Vitamin C tablet you might take may be 50 milligrams (50 mg). A milligram is a thousandth of a gram.

- Time periods can be counted by their numbers of seconds or parts of a second. For scientific purposes, no ordinary clock is accurate enough to determine the second. So the second is defined as the time it takes for a certain form of the chemical caesium 133 to send out 9,192,631,770 (just over 9 billion) wave lengths of radiation.

THE LUCK OF THE DICE

Many computers have random number generators. They produce a sequence of numbers by chance, with no order or pattern. The sequence does not repeat itself. A simple version of this is the die. Throw a die one hundred times, and keep a record of the numbers that come up. Does each number, from 1 to 6, come up about the same number of times? Is there any pattern to the numbers?

TIME-NUMBER MACHINES

The clock is a time-based number machine — it tells the time in numbers. The stopwatch measures short amounts of time very accurately. Use a stopwatch to time a simple action, such as clapping your hands twenty times. Try it a few times. Does your time get shorter? Electronic digital stopwatches show the time in numbers and can measure times to hundredths and thousandths of a second. These can be observed at sports events.

The first practical mechanical calculator was based on the same principle. It was invented by Blaise Pascal (*see page 40*). To run it, the operator turned a handle. Gottfried Leibniz improved the design to make a machine that could multiply, by adding the same number several times. This led to an entire range of mechanical calculators operated by handles and levers. Early in the twentieth century, calculators started to be commonly run by electric motors.

During the 1830s, Charles Babbage's designs for mechanical calculators were complicated. He had an idea for a machine that could do various types of calculations according to different sequences of instructions fed into it in the form of patterns of holes punched in cards. This idea was taken up again in the 1940s. But instead of mechanical devices, such as switches and levers, the newer devices used tiny pulses of electricity. These were the first electronic computers.

Today, computers are everywhere, working not only with numbers but with letters, symbols, words, pictures, sounds, and even ideas. Yet inside such a computing machine, numbers rule. The computer's basic language is numerical. It uses the binary number system, based on 2s. A tiny pulse of electricity ("on") represents 1, and no electricity ("off") represents 0. Using this simple system, combined in more and more complicated ways, a computer or calculator can accomplish difficult tasks, including those based on advanced scientific ideas, in a fraction of a second.

Large computer networks are essential in the business world today. Information from around the world is accessible. This information changes quickly and affects the decisions people make.

DIY SCIENCE

THE ASCII CODES

If you page through a computer book or manual, you will probably find the word *ASCII* (pronounced "askey") and perhaps a chart of ASCII codes. ASCII is the American Standard Code for Information Interchange. A computer can work only with numbers. So it changes all characters (the numerals, letters, signs, and symbols on the keyboard) into numbers using the ASCII codes to manipulate and record and change them. ASCII has 128 main codes. A selection is shown below.

THE "HEX" CODES

If you see rows of letters and numbers on a computer screen, like 1B 3F 4C 2E, these are probably programming codes

Character	ASCII code	Hexadecimal code	Binary code
$	036	24	0100100
*	042	2A	0101010
1	049	31	0110001
2	050	32	0110010
3	051	33	0110011
;	059	3B	0111011
?	063	3F	0111111
A	065	41	1000001
B	066	42	1000010
C	067	43	1000011
a	097	61	1100001
b	098	62	1100010
c	099	63	1100011
~	126	7E	1111110

- The early computer ENIAC could work at the rate of about three hundred number calculations per second. A modern supercomputer does more than four billion calculations per second.

- ENIAC would fill all the rooms of an average family house. It would also be warm to the touch. It used the same amount of electricity required for two hundred one-kilowatt electric heaters.

- ENIAC was programmed not by pressing keys on a keyboard or by feeding in a magnetic disk, but by changing the wiring connections between its different parts.

- ENIAC was a great advance over the previous mechanical devices and remained in use for ten years.

in the hexadecimal number system *(see page 19)*. This system is based on 16s. The numbers that represent letters, numerals, and other characters are in binary form inside the computer. Binary numbers can be written in a shortened way using the normal decimal system, but even shorter in hexadecimal. The number 1111111 in binary is the same as the number 127 in decimal and 7F in hexadecimal.

NUMBER MACHINES EVERYWHERE

The small size of electronic circuits allows them to be used in more and more machines and devices. The circuits process numbers and information and count, calculate, and control. Look for evidence of them in watches, calculators, measuring devices, radios, compact disc and cassette tape players, televisions, ovens, washing machines, cars, and many more places.

A "HOLE" LOT OF INFORMATION

Before the era of electronics, many computers and similar machines were controlled by punch cards or paper tape. The positions and patterns of the holes in the cards or tape carried instructions telling the machine what to do. The same system was used to record information on cards. For instance, an automobile dealership had a card for each type of car it had for sale. The various features of each type of car were recorded using hole punches in cards. Pushing rods through the holes in a pile of cards selected the cars with those particular features.

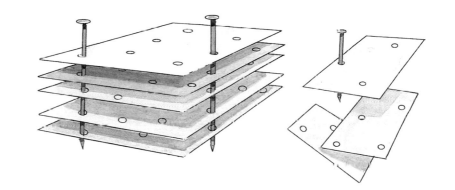

NUMBERS IN THE FUTURE

We have been using the decimal system of numbers for several centuries. By international agreement, all modern scientific measuring and recording is based on it. Yet each civilization, such as the ancient Babylonians, the Chinese, and the Mayans of Central America, were just as familiar with their own number systems. They were equally at home counting in 60s or 20s, rather than 10s as we do. Probably they could not imagine changing their number system. Can you imagine learning a new set of numerals and a new number system in the future?

GLOSSARY

algebra — an area of mathematics that deals with amounts or numbers by means of general symbols, like x and y, and with finding the values of unknown numbers by calculating them from known quantities.

arithmetic — the process of doing calculations with numbers.

binary system — a number system based on twos. It is used in computing and is the simplest number system.

calculus — an area of mathematics that deals with amounts and quantities that change over time.

cardinal number — a number that is used in simple counting.

circumference — the measurement all the way around a circle.

constant — a number that is always the same, such as the speed of light.

decimal system — a number system that is based on tens.

diameter — the longest distance across a circle.

ellipse — an oval shape that has two centers.

fraction — a part or portion of the whole.

geometry — the branch of mathematics that uses numbers to describe lines and shapes.

hieroglyph — a character (picture-word or symbol) used in a system of ancient writing.

infinity — a quantity that is greater than any assignable quantity. Infinity does not go on forever.

mean — in mathematics, a term that identifies the average.

median — the middle number in a sequence of numbers.

mode — in data involving numbers, the number that comes up most often.

ordinal number — a number that shows position or rank in a series or sequence.

percent — per one hundred. For example, 40 out of 100 is 40 percent.

prime number — a number that cannot be divided by any whole numbers except by itself or the number 1.

radius — the distance from the center to the circumference of a circle.

ratio — a comparison of one number to another.

tessellation — a regular, repeated shape.

theory of relativity — Albert Einstein's theory that there is no absolute motion in the Universe, only relative motion. This theory shows that we live not in a flat space and uniform, absolute time of everyday experience but in a place of curved space-time.

topology — a branch of geometry that deals with how objects change when bent, twisted, and turned inside out.

WEB SITES

www.geocities.com/CapeCanaveral/6747/

www.ncsa.uiuc.edu/SDG/Experimental/vatican.exhibit/exhibit/d-mathematics/Mathematics.html

www.essex1.com/people/speer/metric.html

www.maths.tcd.ie/pub/HistMath/HistMath.html

www.gre.ac.uk/~aj434/

BOOKS

Abacus Made Easy. M. Davidow
  (American Printing House)

Algebra Acrobatic Puzzles. Morris Bureloff
  (Activity Resources)

Algebra in Concrete. Mary Laycock and Reuben
  Schadler (Activity Resources)

Calculators, Number Patterns, and Magic.
  Morris Bureloff and Connie Johnson
  (Activity Resources)

Calculus by and for Young People. Donald Cohen
  (D. Cohen Mathman)

Compute a Design (series). Patricia Wright
  (Jacobs)

Computer Confusion. Beth Cruise
  (Simon and Schuster Children's)

Computers of the Future. David A. Darling
  (Silver Burdett)

Counting on Frank. Rod Clement
  (Gareth Stevens)

Fractions. S. Harold Collins (Garlic Press)

Fractions and Decimals. K. Bryant-Mole (EDC)

Geometry in Our World. John Engelhardt
  (NCTM)

Kids Can! (series). *The Kids' Science Book.*
  Robert Hirschfeld and Nancy White
  (Gareth Stevens)

Measure Up With Science (series).
  Brenda Walpole (Gareth Stevens)

Metric Measure. Ron Marson (Tops Learning)

Metrics at Work. John L. McCabe (Garlic Press)

Record Breakers (series). *Machines and Inventions.*
  Peter Lafferty (Gareth Stevens)

VIDEOS

A Plus B Squared. (International Film Bureau)

Algebraic Factoring. (Multi-Media Mathematics)

Area and Volume. (Journal Films and Video)

Basic Math: Fractions and Decimals. (Bergwall)

Beginning Algebra. (Great Plains National
  Instructional Television Library)

The Case of the Law of Averages.
  (Agency for Instructional Technology)

Descartes and Problem Solving.
  (American Mathematical Society)

Fractions and Some Cool Distractions. (Rahlic)

How to Read a Financial Statement. (RMI Media)

PLACES TO VISIT

Carnegie Science Center
One Allegheny Avenue
Pittsburgh, PA 15212

Miami Museum of Science
3280 South Miami Avenue
Miami, FL 33129

Science Center of British Columbia
1455 Quebec Street
Vancouver, British Columbia V6A 3Z7

Science Museum of Minnesota
30 East Tenth Street
St. Paul, MN 55101

INDEX